AF867761

MY

5 MILLION DOLLAR

TSP

FEDERAL RETIREMENT

By Abraham Grungold

Publisher Abraham Grungold

www.Grungold.com

ISBN 979-8-234-14586-4

Publisher: Abraham Grungold

Publisher's Link: www.Grungold.com

Dedication

"To my Mom and Dad:

“Thank you for teaching me how to work hard for every dollar and how to save for a rainy day."

"This book was written with the assistance of Google AI (Gemini). Gemini was utilized for brainstorming, structuring, and copy-editing the text. The ultimate voice, analysis, and content remain my own." AI also assisted with the process of how to publish a book.

A special thank you to my former federal co-worker and loyal friend, Bob Lee. He was instrumental with the proof editing and providing constructive criticism.

Epigraph

Financial success can easily be achieved; it only takes a little effort.
Abraham Grungold

Table of Contents

Introduction

I wrote this book because I hope that it will help every federal employee and retiree to become a TSP Millionaire. During my first TSP meeting in 1987, I was confident that I could achieve this milestone during my federal career.

I am sharing my journey, my strategies and my psyche of how I achieved this. The book is simply to educate readers who are in the government or those who left the government on how financial success can be achieved.

Some ideas, suggestions and warnings are repeated throughout the book. This was done intentionally to reinforce the important messages the book has to offer. I wish everyone who reads it good luck.

Chapter 1
The Stone Age of the Thrift Saving Plan.

Empowering Your Financial Future.

Federal agencies provide employees with the documents required to understand human resource policies, travel regulations, ethics, and cyber security threats. However, when it comes to the Federal Employee Retirement System (FERS) and the Thrift Savings Plan (TSP), employees must seek out information on their own.

Because each person has unique needs and concerns— a single person faces different variables than a married couple with children—your plan of action must factor in your specific situation. Navigating the long road to retirement with informed choices can empower you and ultimately add hundreds or thousands of dollars to your future nest egg.

The Resources to Navigate the Vast Amount of Information.

Acquiring the basic information to comprehend FERS and grow your TSP does not require an exorbitant amount of time. It is never too early in your federal career to expose yourself to the vast amount of knowledge available on the Office of Personnel Management (OPM) and the TSP websites. Familiarizing yourself with these basics early ensure you will not feel overwhelmed by later financial choices or FERS retirement milestones.

The following resources are highly useful when researching TSP issues:

- TSP website makes it easy to review statements, interfund transfers and investment allocations. The website separates many sections and topics.
- TSP Newsletter: Covers TSP performance and system changes. (Free at TSP.gov)

- TSP Webinars: Offers informative sessions on various retirement topics. (Free at TSP.gov)

My Journey from the Health Care Industry to Federal Service. Seeking Career Stability.

On November 12, 1985, I began my federal career with the U.S. Department of Labor's Pension Welfare Benefit Administration in Boston, MA. My starting salary was $21,804—a $12,000 pay decrease from my previous position as a Medical Technologist at Union Hospital in Lynn, MA.

Despite the temporary financial setback, I viewed government employment as a vast opportunity to work for a secure organization. During the 1980s, Union Hospital was undergoing frequent mergers and financial restructurings, and I did not see a future there. Today, that hospital has been demolished to make room for a commercial project.

Navigating the FERS Transition.

When I started my federal service, the TSP did not yet exist; it was introduced later in July 1987. I initially entered service under the Civil Service Retirement System (CSRS). However, an OPM policy mandated that any employee hired after January 1, 1984, would automatically be transitioned into the new FERS retirement system.

The structural difference between the two systems was stark. While the CSRS system provided a retirement annuity worth two-thirds of your salary, the FERS system paid out approximately one-third. The government expected federal employees to utilize the TSP to save enough funds to make up the missing one-third difference.

Early Financial Adaptations.

Prior to joining the government, my retirement savings consisted of a local bank IRA and a defined benefit plan from the hospital. As the federal government rolled out FERS, they also promoted the payroll U.S. Savings Bond Program. Although not an official retirement plan, it was an excellent vehicle for tax-deferred investing.

I immediately signed up for the payroll savings program. I started by purchasing $50 bonds and quickly scaled up to buying $1,000 bonds to accelerate my savings.

The Spark that Began My TSP Millionaire Journey.

The TSP 5% Employer Matching Contribution and a Vision.

In July 1987, OPM representatives visited federal offices to present the newly launched TSP. Armed with charts, their message was clear: employees needed to contribute to the TSP to supplement the reduced FERS annuity, and the government would provide a 5% matching contribution to help them do so. They emphasized that over a 30-year federal career, an employee could become a TSP Millionaire.

Holding a bachelor's degree in accounting and a master's degree in finance, a light bulb went off in my head. I knew right then that I could achieve that million-dollar milestone by the end of my career. Interestingly, I was the only person in my office excited by the presentation. My coworkers were all legacy CSRS employees; they were restricted to contributing just 5% of their salaries and received no government matching funds.

Overcoming Cash Flow Constraints.

As a newer employee with less than five years of service, I faced strict investment restrictions. Most contributions had to be directed into the Government Bond Fund (G Fund). While the Common Stock Fund (C Fund) and Fixed Corporate Bond Fund (F Fund) existed, we were restricted from using them until hitting the five-year service milestone.

Federal employees could contribute up to 10% of their salary, but during the initial startup phase, a 2-to-3-month "catchup phase" allowed us to contribute 15% since we hadn't been investing all year. This posed a serious challenge for me. Earning roughly $29,000 per year while managing a tight budget for a newly purchased condominium meant that a 15% contribution rate left me unable to pay monthly bills. To protect my cash flow and supplement my income during those lean early years, I continued working my hospital job on weekends and holidays.

Mastering the Mechanics by Deciphering the Plan Documents.

My professional role with the Department of Labor involved investigating pension retirement plans very similar to the TSP. In that line of work, the most critical step is reading the baseline plan document. Naturally, I read the TSP handbook as soon as I became an investor.

Although it was only 20 to 30 pages long, understanding the mechanics of how the plan worked was vital. As a new employee, I wanted to know my maximum contribution limits. And I wanted to understand how and when I could allocate among the available funds.

Gathering this information back then required patience. We did not have email and there was no TSP website, so asking human resources a question about the TSP, meant calling someone on the phone who usually didn't know the answers because the plan was entirely new to them. Turning to co-workers for TSP advice was a waste of time since the FERS-specific features of the TSP did not apply to their CSRS rules. Reading the TSP handbook was critical to my success.

The Paperwork Era.

Reaching five years of federal service finally allowed me to invest in any fund at any percentage from 0% to 100%, and I began experimenting with all the options. However, executing changes in the early days of the TSP moved at a turtle's pace.

A contribution change or an interfund transfer took up to three weeks to complete. You had to manually fill out a form, submit it to your human resource representative, and wait for them to mail it to the TSP office in New Orleans. Weeks later, you would receive a physical copy of the form, date-stamped to confirm when the transaction was officially executed.

Tracking Progress Before the Internet.

Account transparency was also a slow process during this pre-internet, pre-email era. To find out your account balance, you had to wait for the detailed statements which were only mailed out in July and December.

These biannual printouts detailed your deposited contributions, investment growth, and government matching funds. I spent hours reviewing these comprehensive statements to reconcile the numbers with my biweekly earnings and leave statements. Because employee contributions and interfund transfers took several weeks to reflect in the system, nothing was immediate. It required deep patience and consistent attention to detail.

Today, everything is instantaneous. Contribution allocations, interfund transfers, loans and account balance can be reviewed immediately and transacted in a day.

Chapter 2

Myths Surrounding the Thrift Saving Plan.

Myth 1: You Must Be a High Earner to Become a TSP Millionaire.

For many years, federal employees have claimed, "I can never be a millionaire because I am not a high wage earner." That is false. Many believe they must earn over $100,000 per year to achieve a seven-figure Thrift Savings Plan (TSP) balance.

My own career disproves this. During my first 11 years of federal service, I never earned above $50,000. For my first 20 years of federal service, my salary never exceeded $100,000. Yet, strategic investing allowed me to reach the millionaire milestone.

Myth 2: TSP Loans Are the Worst Financial Decision.

Many financial advisors claim that taking out a TSP loan is the worst thing you can do. That is false. When managed correctly, a TSP loan can be a powerful tool.

When TSP loans first became available in the 1990s, the application process took several weeks. Initially, these loans were free, which unfortunately led employees to treat their accounts like ATMs. To curb this high volume, the TSP instituted a $50 application fee in the 2000s. The loan interest rate was—and still is—equivalent to the G Fund rate. There are personal loans and residential loans. Each one has specific rules that are dictated by the TSP.

During my federal career, I utilized four TSP loans effectively:

- First Loan (2000): A personal $17,000 loan at 5.65% interest to purchase a car. I paid it off in less than two years.
- Second Loan (2002): A $50,000 res-

identential loan at less than 6% interest. I paid it off within four years.

- Third Loan (2004): A $34,000 personal loan to purchase another property, taking advantage of the rule allowing two outstanding loans at once. I paid it off in under five years.
- Fourth Loan (2014): A $21,000 personal loan at less than 6% interest, to purchase a car. I paid it off in less than two years.

Each loan carried a low interest rate tied to the G Fund. Instead of paying interest to Toyota Finance Company or Bank of America, I paid that interest back to myself. I also accelerated my payment schedules, frequently requesting payoff amounts to clear the debt early. The interest and principal payments were paid back to my TSP account and reinvested in the G Fund.

Myth 3: You Must Pay Off TSP Loans Before You Retire.

Another common misconception is that

you must completely pay off your TSP loans before separating from federal service. That is false.

The SECURE Act 2.0 introduced provisions allowing federal employees to carry their TSP loans into retirement, offering a variety of repayment methods. If you choose to stop making payments, the outstanding balance will be treated as a distribution. In that scenario, you will owe income taxes and potential Internal Revenue Service (IRS) early withdrawal penalties.

Myth 4: You Can Become a Millionaire by Investing Solely in the G Fund.

Some employees believe they can build a million-dollar nest egg using only the safest fund. For the vast majority of feds, that is false.

If you have a standard 20-to-30-year federal career, the G Fund alone will not get you there. There are extreme exceptions. If you plan to work 40-50 years for the federal government and you contribute a significant amount of your salary, you could possibly reach a million-dollar balance by solely investing in the G Fund. If your career is shorter than 40 years, you cannot rely solely on the G Fund to achieve this goal.

Myth 5: You Must Invest in All the TSP Funds to Grow Your Money Faster.

Diversifying across every single fund is often preached as a necessity. That is false.

You do not need to hold every fund to maximize growth.

Over my career, I experimented with the G, C, S, I, and F Funds. I did well, but I also monitored market conditions to know when to exit. For instance, when the stock market is booming, you do not want your money tied up in corporate bonds via the F Fund. Similarly, if international markets are struggling, you should avoid the I Fund. Ultimately, simplicity wins: if you choose to invest exclusively in the C Fund, the TSP history data shows you can become a TSP millionaire in 25 to 30 years.

Myth 6: You Must Take Withdrawals Immediately Upon Retirement.

Many employees assume retirement automatically triggers mandatory account distributions. That is false.

There are no mandatory withdrawals simply because you retired from federal service. If you hold a Traditional TSP, you are subject to Required Minimum Distributions (RMDs). For most retirees, RMDs do not begin until you reach age 73.

Myth 7: You Must Transfer Your Previous 401(k) Into the TSP.

When entering federal service, employees often think they are required to consolidate their old retirement accounts into the government plan. That is false.

While the TSP allows you to roll over qualified traditional 401(k) funds from previous employers, it is entirely optional. In my case, I held a retirement account with a prior employer that was a non-qualified plan, meaning it could not transfer into the TSP. Instead, I successfully rolled it into a private

Individual Retirement Account (IRA). My prior employer's retirement account was a 403(b). And my rollover balance to my IRA was less than 5,000 dollars.

Myth 8: You Can Avoid Required Minimum Distributions (RMDs) entirely.

The rules around RMDs can confuse investors, but the truth depends entirely on your account type.

- Traditional TSP (True): You are required to take RMDs starting at your required age.
- Roth TSP (True): No RMDs are required. Thanks to updated tax laws, you are no longer required to take RMDs from a Roth TSP during your lifetime.

Myth 9: Other Retirement Accounts Offer the Same Loan Flexibility.

The TSP allows for one outstanding loan of up to $50,000, which can be repaid over a five-year plan for a simple $50 application fee requested online. Believing this flexibility exists elsewhere is false. Private IRAs strictly prohibit loans. Furthermore, private-sector 401(k) plans are not required to offer loans; it is an optional provision left entirely to the discretion of individual employers. My 403(b) with my prior employer did not provide any loan provisions.

The Limitations of the TSP Bureaucracy.

While the modern TSP platform introduced helpful updates in 2022—including expanded fund windows and digital assistance—the system lacks flexibility. Empathy is not the TSP Board's priority.

Decades ago, Burger King popularized the slogan, "Have it your way," emphasizing that special orders did not upset them. Throughout my federal career, management similarly told me, "If you need help, just ask."

Unfortunately, the Federal Retirement Thrift Investment Board does not accommodate its members with that same spirit.

During a financial crisis, the Board refuses to bend its rules—not for personal financial hardships, nor for a global pandemic. While the CARES Act did provide relief during COVID, it only pertained to penalty-free withdrawals, not loan restructuring.

The TSP should offer exceptions for its participants. For example, one of my clients faced a financial hardship and he was eager to pay the application fee and borrow his *own* money, yet he was trapped by rigid timelines. The TSP should grant a one-time waiver for the strict 60-day loan re-application waiting period. No one likes asking for help, but during times of severe financial distress, the Board could grant these waivers to alleviate the emotional and economic burdens on its members.

I always said that the government can do anything with the stroke of a pen.

Joining the Elite 3% TSP Millionaires.

There are approximately 7 million participants in the Thrift Savings Plan, yet only about 3% have reached millionaire status. This elite group consists of employees who contributed consistently throughout their entire careers, invested aggressively, and weathered every macroeconomic storm—including the COVID-19 market crash—without fear.

It is an elite club, but it is one that constantly welcomes new members. To join them, you must tune out the noise and ignore the common misconceptions.

As a final reminder, you do not need to do any of the following to achieve wealth:

- You do not have to contribute the maximum allowed by the IRS if your monthly budget cannot sustain it.
- You do not have to roll over private 401(k) money into the TSP.
- You do not have to time the market using frequent interfund transfers.

Success comes down to employee contributions, time, and letting the stock market do the heavy lifting for you.

Chapter 3
The Strategy to become a TSP millionaire.

The "Let It Ride" Philosophy.

To become a TSP millionaire or multi-millionaire, it has nothing to do with skill or luck. Investing in any of the TSP funds is not gambling. But if you are jumping from fund to fund trying to time the markets' fluctuations, that is simply a recipe for disaster. As an old federal colleague of mine who is also a successful TSP investor would say, "Just Let It Ride."

Again, as I previously mentioned, when I started in the TSP at its inception in 1987, there was no computer technology for checking your daily balance. Making a simple interfund transfer took several weeks to accomplish. It was all done manually by mailing forms and receiving paper statements. Furthermore, for employees with less than five years of federal service, there were strict limitations on which funds you could invest in.

The Sacrifices Behind the First Million.

My journey to becoming a TSP multi-millionaire is not just about making contributions and investing aggressively; it is about making the sacrifice to contribute the maximum very single day of my federal career. In the early years, the maximum contribution allowed was 10% of your salary. I started my federal career earning $21,804 per year, and during my first 11 years of service, I never earned more than $50,000 per year.

To afford necessities like food, housing, and clothing while maximizing my retirement allocations, I worked a second, part-time job outside of federal service. I did not deny myself the pleasures of life—I still traveled and played golf—but I strictly lived on a budget. Long before my federal career even began, I practiced the concept of "Paying Yourself First" by contributing to a personal, long-term investment IRA. I maintained these habits by never spending more than what was in my bank account and purchasing a modest home that I could easily afford.

Milestones and Surviving the Rollercoaster.

Over my 36-year federal career, I achieved many wonderful accolades, but hitting the multi-million-dollar mark was my greatest achievement as a federal employee. The path required navigating two distinct archetypes of TSP participants: those who ride the "Merry-Go-Round" of the risk-free G Fund, and those who choose the "Rollercoaster" of the C, S, I, F, and Lifecycle funds. The G Fund offers stability, but its rate of return historically fails to keep pace with inflation. If you are withdrawing 4% per year while the G Fund only earns 3%, your account will steadily diminish. To build true wealth, you must embrace the rollercoaster.

My milestones highlight the rewards of staying the course:

The First Million (May 2014):

This milestone took me 27 years of consistent accumulation. Along the way, I weathered the 2000 Dot-Com boom and the 2008 Financial Crisis, during which my account progressively dropped by 40% before fully recovering in 2014.

The Second Million (February 2019):

Achieved just five years later. I contributed the IRS maximum, included over-age-50 catch-up contributions, and rode a rapidly growing stock market while remaining aggressively split between the C and S Funds.

The Third Million (December 2021):

Appendix A

Accomplished in a mere 22 months. By this point, I had consolidated my holdings solely into the C Fund, finding it less volatile than the S Fund. When the COVID-19 pandemic hit in 2020, my portfolio quickly depreciated by 35%, but I kept buying cheaper units via payroll contributions—utilizing dollar-cost averaging—allowing the balance to skyrocket when the market bounced back.

During July 1987 to February 2022, these were my contributing years in the TSP. I contributed **less than** 400,000 dollars during this time period.

The Fourth Million (June 2025):

Appendix B

I retired from federal service in February 2022 right at the three-million-dollar mark, having utilized four TSP loans (two personal, two residential) over my career. Even after retirement, I continued investing in the C Fund. I started making TSP monthly withdrawals which started at 4,500 dollars per month and subsequently increasing those TSP withdrawals to 5,000 dollars per month. In February 2025, after completing my 2024 Federal Tax return, I stopped making TSP withdrawals because I did not need the funds and it was putting me in a very high tax bracket. The 2024 presidential election was making me nervous. During October 2024, when the financial markets reached an all-time high, I moved my entire 3.6-million-dollar TSP balance into the G Fund.

In April 2025, I decided to take advantage of the Tariff Crisis, and I moved my 3.6 -million-dollar G Fund balance into the C and S Funds. I did this with four interfund transfers during April and May 2025. The financial markets had taken a significant drop due to the Tariff Crisis and the continuation of the 2022 Ukrainian War. The financial markets began to rebound and in June 2025 my TSP balance reached 4 million dollars.

The Fifth Million (June 2026):

Appendix C

Even though the Iran War began in February 2026, and the financial markets were taking a significant dip, I continued to invest 50 percent in the C and 50 percent in the S Fund. I anticipated that this financial dip in the markets would only last a few months. After a few months the financial markets showed signs of rebounding. I reached my ultimate milestone of $5 million dollars in June 2026.

My TSP experience, patience and aggressive investment strategy resulted in my TSP to grow from 3.6 million to 5 million (1.4 million) in just 14 months. At this time, I have not changed my TSP investment mix of 50% C Fund and 50% S Fund.

The Simple Recipe for Financial Success.

Again, out of the millions of active and retired TSP participants, only about 3% belong to the elite "TSP Millionaires Club." These are ordinary public servants who lacked massive salaries but possessed immense patience. The basic recipe relies on five core pillars:

1. **Maximize Contributions:** Always contribute what you can afford. At a bare minimum, invest the 5% re-

quired to capture the full government matching contribution. Failing to do so is the equivalent of turning down a free 5% annual raise or bonus. As your salary increases over time, systematically bump your contributions to 11%, 13%, 15%, and eventually to the absolute IRS maximum.

2. **Invest Aggressively:** True growth demands equity exposure. While I briefly experimented with the international stocks and bonds of the I Fund, I ultimately focused long-term on the C Fund (which mirrors the S&P 500) and the S Fund (which tracks the broader market completions outside the S&P 500, to include the NASDAQ). If you lack investment knowledge, Lifecycle (L) Funds can act as an effective automatic pilot.

3. **Patience and Time:** Compounding interest requires a 20-to-30-year horizon to work its magic. Do not view the TSP as a short-term, "quick

in-and-out" investment tool.

4. **Ignore Financial Crises:** Maintain total emotional discipline when market corrections occur. Volatility is an intrinsic element of the stock market. When a steep downward trend hits, close your eyes to the sensationalized financial news cycle to curb anxiety. Understand that a dip represents a temporary depreciation in value, not a permanent realized loss— unless you panic and transfer your money into the G Fund at the absolute bottom. Treat market drops like an "Amazon Prime Day Sale" to accumulate cheaper fund units.

5. **Seek Credible Mentorship:** Tune out unverified, anonymous advice found on Facebook forums or informal blogs where self-proclaimed experts predict recessions. Instead, seek out peer mentors or senior personnel within your own federal agency who have actually achieved millionaire status and understand

the real nuances of the system. Find a federal employee or federal retiree who is also a TSP millionaire. They have done it and they can help you.

Pitfalls to Avoid

To protect your retirement future, active employees and retirees alike must consciously avoid five critical blunders:

- **Under-contributing**: Leaving matching dollars on the table. For example, an employee earning a $100,000 salary who only contributes 4% loses $1,000 of free matching funds every single year.
- **Crowdsourcing Financial Advice**: Taking financial cues from complete strangers online who refuse to share their own portfolios or real track records.
- **Market Timing**: Attempting to jump in and out of funds based on short-term fear, which frequently

traps investors into buying high and selling low.

- **Defaulting to Annuities:** Annuitizing your hard-earned TSP balance, which strips away your financial flexibility and can severely limit overall retirement income compared to personal withdrawal strategies.
- **Neglecting TSP Loans:** Failing to timely repay outstanding TSP loans, which automatically triggers a taxable distribution event, resulting in heavy penalties and permanent loss of retirement growth.

Lastly, be highly cautious of financial advisers charging steep commissions, such as a 1.5% management fee. On a million-dollar balance, that translates to a $15,000 annual fee out of your pocket with absolutely zero guarantee of performance. Remember, managing your own TSP, there are no management fees or commissions.

Why Hitting the Mark Matters.

Many federal employees focus entirely on paying off their credit cards and mortgages early while treating retirement savings as a secondary goal; this is a critical mistake. Living on a budget and trimming minor daily expenses, like your Starbucks coffee or restaurant lunches, is a small price to pay for what your TSP balance will look like with these cost savings methods.

A million-dollar TSP balance serves three crucial functions during your retirement years:

1. **Supplementing Fixed Annuities.**

Even with a steady Federal Employees Retirement System (FERS) annuity and a monthly Social Security benefit, your fixed income may not fully cover everyday lifestyle inflation and dynamic living expenses. A healthy TSP allows you to make structured monthly withdrawals to safely bridge that gap.

2. Funding Unplanned Life Events and Long-Term Care.

Life inevitably throws curveballs in retirement, such as funding a grandchild's college education, handling steep pharmaceutical needs, or taking out a mortgage on a second vacation home. Most important, your TSP acts as an essential insurance policy for long-term clinical care. If you or your spouse requires an assisted living facility or a nursing home, current annual rates range from $75,000 to $150,000 per year. A robust TSP protects your family's assets from being completely erased by round-the-clock medical care.

3. Prevent outliving your money.

If you retire at age 62 and systematically withdraw a conservative $30,000 per year, a million-dollar balance is structured to easily last 33 years. Even when managed conservatively throughout your post-retirement life, your principal will remain highly secure well past age 95, ensuring that you can travel, remodel your home, and enjoy your lifestyle without the lingering fear of running completely out of funds.

Conclusion: Decoupled from the Hype.

The Thrift Savings Plan remains an extraordinary, low-cost investment system that truly gives federal employees the best bang for their buck. It is beautifully insulated from the annoying, high-pressure solicitations, daily emails, and spam phone calls pushing gold coins, annuities, or crypto assets that will hound you from commercial brokerages and sales representatives.

While it is entirely appropriate to eventually transition your assets into alternative structures if you are executing complex estate plans or establishing charitable legacy distributions, the core formula for the vast majority of your career remains unchanged. Adopt an investment strategy that matches your personal risk tolerance, ignore the short-term panic of the crowd, utilize the wealth of historical research tools directly on the official TSP website, and always continue to Pay Yourself First.

Chapter 4

Why do TSP Investors become Millionaires and others do not?

Again, among the seven million active federal employees and retirees investing in the TSP, you find two distinct types of investors: the long-term Rollercoaster Riders and the short-term Merry-Go-Rounders.

The Rollercoaster Riders handle the ups and downs of the market. They are aggressive risk-takers who invest heavily in the stock-indexed C, S, and I Funds. Regardless of how volatile or scary the ride gets, they stay the course, buckle up, and rarely make interfund transfers. They understand that while the ride can be bumpy, the TSP historically bounces back and grows over time. Because they realize that without risk there is no reward, these investors typically become self-made TSP millionaires.

The Merry-Go-Rounders invest solely in the G Fund. There is no risk; they enjoy a smooth, easy ride going around in a circle and listening to the festive music. They sleep great at night knowing their account balance will not fluctuate. The trade-off is that there is very little growth potential. Investing an entire career strictly in the G Fund will typically only provide a retirement balance of approximately $250,000. The only way a Merry-Go Rounder can hit the million-dollar mark is to maintain a high federal salary, stay employed for 40 to 50 years, and let sheer time do the heavy lifting.

There is nothing wrong with either approach. Risk is different for everyone. It is a matter of personal choice, recognizing your own risk tolerance, and finding the path that lets you sleep at night. I am reminded of people who swap recipes: I might make my dish with oregano and thyme, while you might make that exact same dish with dill and basil. Just like you can make a great meal in different ways, you can achieve financial success through various avenues.

Interestingly, many Merry-Go-Rounders are only conservative within the TSP; outside of government, they may hold equities in an IRA or brokerage account, choosing simply to treat their TSP as a safe haven. Whichever ride you prefer, the most important thing is that you feel comfortable. It is your money, and it is your decision.

I had invested my TSP and my IRA aggressively. This means I invested in 100 percent equities among both accounts. As a young person this approach is fine because you have many years to retire. As a senior person, this approach is highly risky. But I still see a great deal of growth in the market. Also, my entire portfolio of investments and assets are not in stock equities.

The Psychology of the Crash.

Being human, market declines—however brief—tend to take on outsized importance in the survivor part of our brains. While we all know past performance does not guarantee future results, a lot of people get nervous very quickly when a downturn lasts for a while. Merry-go rounds are simply less stressful than rollercoasters.

Yet, the data on the ever-growing club of TSP millionaires shows they share a common trait: the ability to hang on during a bumpy ride. This group includes people of all ages, backgrounds, educations, and jobs. Most invested heavily in stock index funds for an average of 29 years. They stuck with the C, S, and I fund during hard times like the 2008–2009 Great Recession, while others fled to the "safe" harbor of the G Fund—and stayed there, missing out on record bull markets. Investors who continued to buy C and S funds during downturns did exceptionally well because they bought shares on sale during the market dips.

The TSP has always been subject to these cycles. Since I began investing in 1987, several major crises have shaken domestic and international markets:

- Black Friday (1987)
- Dot-com Crisis (2000)
- Financial Crisis of 2008
- Brexit Crisis
- COVID Crisis
- Tariff Crisis
- Ukrainian-Russian War Crisis
- Iranian Crisis

A View from the Front Row.

Over my 36-year federal career—and 39 years as a TSP investor—I was in the plan from the very beginning. I survived many furloughs, which never had a long-term effect on the markets, and rode many different rollercoasters. In the early days, my co-workers and I would spend our lunches discussing where to invest. Back then, our only choices were the G, C, F, and I Funds—a small fraction of current TSP offerings. Because there was no historical track record, I experimented with all of them.

During most of those epic events, I basically did nothing with my investment mix. If I did anything at all, I bought more shares when the value of the funds was spiraling downward. I was always confident that the TSP would rise to higher levels than before the crisis occurred. After 2008, I began focusing on a few strategies.

In May of 2014, I officially became a TSP millionaire.

Knowing I had at least another 8 to 10 years of federal service, I continued to invest aggressively in both the C and S Funds. By 2019, I achieved multi-millionaire status.

Around that time, I shifted to investing solely in the C Fund, finding it offered incredible growth with less volatility than the S Fund.

Then came the COVID crisis of 2020—the scariest ride of them all. The uncertainty was intense, and the first drop caused my

TSP to depreciate 35% within a few short weeks. Remember, depreciation means a temporary decrease in value, not a permanent loss. It was a violent ride with sudden 5% inclines and 10% drops.

When I officially retired from federal service in February 2022, I walked out the door as a TSP multi-millionaire, crossing the three-million-dollar mark. Reaching that milestone stayed with me as my greatest achievement as a federal employee. Today, I work as a full-time financial coach, helping clients who are either TSP millionaires or wish to be. Also, I have guided TSP investors to be TSP multi-millionaires even when they entered retirement.

Even Experts Get Scared: My $400,000 Mistake.

In retirement, my TSP continued to grow far beyond my expectations. Yet, even as my long-term view on the economy remained optimistic, short-term fear eventually got a hold of me, too.

In the fall of 2024, I became deeply concerned about the historical volatility that often plagues the markets, during the month of October. I was also worried that the upcoming 2024 Presidential Election would trigger a severe negative reaction with my TSP balance. Compounding my anxiety, my wife was worried about our balance decreasing and actively encouraged me to protect it. On October 1, 2024, I blinked. I broke my own golden rule: I panicked and transferred 100% of my C Fund holdings into the safe harbor of the G Fund.

It was a mistake. Instead of crashing, the stock market climbed steadily throughout October 2024. Had I practiced what I preached and done absolutely nothing, my TSP account would have gained an additional $225,000 in a single month following the presidential election and it continued to grow up to $400,000 which I could have attained by February 2025.

I am not complaining, nor do I want anyone to feel sorry for me. I share this story because it proves a vital point: the TSP has a nearly 40-year history of volatility and letting short-term fear dictate your strategy causes you to sell your shares much too early. Making frantic interfund moves is a recipe for disaster. You will never be able to accurately time the bottom, you will struggle to figure out when to get back into the market aggressively, and you will lock in a recognized loss. I have never heard a single story of someone making money by selling in a down market. Successful investors buy low and sell high.

I then patiently waited for downward trends to find my opportunity to buy back into the C Fund. This opportunity came in April 2025 as explained in detail in the previous chapter. If you let short-term fear rule your decisions, you stand in your own way. This fear will prevent you from leaving the G Fund and becoming aggressive, once again with the other TSP funds.

Analyzing the Iranian Conflict and Market Anxiety.

Today, the geopolitical conflict with Iran is the latest crisis causing friends, acquaintances, and clients to become incredibly nervous. But we must look at the financial realities logically rather than emotionally.

To keep things in perspective, financial analysts at Wells Fargo recently predicted that the S&P 500 could experience a 12% pullback, dropping from roughly 6,800 down to 6,000. Let us recall that in April 2025, the S&P 500 sat at 4,965. Even if the market pulls back to a value of 6,000, it remains 21% higher than it was just 11 months prior. As another financial expert on CNBC recently noted: when missiles fly, it is usually the best time to buy stocks at a discount.

For active employees, this conflict shouldn't be an index of fear; it is a prime buying opportunity to accumulate cheaper shares via dollar-cost averaging. For retirees, my advice is to brew some calming tea, step away from the financial news, and go work on your pickleball game. This conflict is heavily contained, and the market will adapt.

Two Habits Holding Investors Back:

Procrastination and Fear.

Despite the clear path to wealth, why do TSP millionaires make up such a small percentage of total investors? Again, as of recent statistics, there are roughly 225,000 TSP millionaires out of more than 7.2 million account holders. That means this "elite club" still represents less than 3% of all TSP participants.

Every single one of the active federal employees and retirees would love to be a millionaire. The reasons so few make the cut break down to two basic human behaviors that have nothing to do with the stock market: Procrastination and Fear.

During my career across four different federal agencies, I heard the same examples of Procrastination (making excuses not to contribute) over and over: *"I want to pay off my school loans," "I need to save for a house," "I want to travel,"* or *"I need to save for my wedding. I'll start the next open season."* But the golden rule of wealth building is to pay yourself first. If you contribute at least 5% to the TSP, you receive a 5% matching contribution from the government. That is effectively a free 5% annual salary bonus. When I explained to my co-workers that procrastination meant giving up free money, it always got their attention.

The second barrier is Fear (refusing to leave the G Fund). Terrified co-workers would tell me: *"I do not want my balance to decrease by even one dollar," "A recession is coming,"* or *"The other funds are too volatile."* While I completely understood their anxiety—and experienced it firsthand in 2024—staying paralyzed in the G Fund limits your future growth.

Unfortunately, federal agencies are failing to properly educate their staff on this milestone benefit. Instead of teaching employees how to maximize the TSP, agencies often bring in outside financial representatives to annual conferences whose primary goal is to convince employees to move their TSP funds into private companies or high-fee annuities. The government needs to bring in genuine TSP experts who can show employees how to leverage the plan for a successful retirement.

Get-Rich-Quick Schemes Fail.

The TSP Does Not.

Many investors around the world are constantly searching for the next big shortcut to wealth. Throughout my life, I have heard friends, co-workers, and clients rave about a "hot new stock" or a sure thing investment opportunity. Unfortunately, I never had one person come back to tell me they were actually successful.

Look at what happened with GameStop: the stock shot from $65 a share up to $420, and then plummeted right back down to $61, all within a single week. This is the definition of a classic pump-and-dump scheme. The artificial hype surged, but the reality of the stock's actual valuation eventually hit home. Sure, a handful of lucky day-traders made money, but a massive wave of casual investors lost their shirts.

The TSP is the exact opposite of a gamble. Think of an active federal employee earning a modest $50,000 salary who consistently contributes 5% over a 30-year career.

By retirement, they should cross the million-dollar mark.

Over those three decades, they will only have contributed $75,000 of their own hard-earned salary to reach that $1,000,000 balance. When you look at the math, that almost sounds like a get-rich-quick scheme itself: invest $75,000 and walk away with a million! The catch is that it cannot be accomplished quickly. It takes 30 years. But what an incredible payoff.

To put that in perspective, consider an individual who takes out a $75,000 home mortgage. After paying it off over 30 years, do they own a million-dollar piece of real estate? Highly unlikely, real estate is an important pillar of stability, but maximizing your TSP is equally vital.

Real wealth building should be viewed like planting a tree. If you water it, give it rich soil, and allow it to sit in the sunshine, it will eventually grow into something tall, strong, and enduring. The Federal Retirement Thrift Investment Board understands this principle, which is why as of October 2020, all newly hired federal employees are automatically enrolled with a mandatory 5% baseline contribution. This brilliant policy guarantees that employees are immediately placed on the right path toward nurturing their own financial trees from day one.

Actionable Advice for TSP Participants.

Achieving success is one thing, but once you make it to the financial "top," you have to work just as hard to stay there. To maintain your edge, you must embrace a few timeless rules:

- Show Some Patience: You must show patience both with the stock market and with the day-to-day logistics of the TSP, including navigating the website.

- Knowledge is Power: A lot of people have a poor experience simply because they do not take the time to read. You must seek historical stock prices and financial information directly from the source. Read the newsletters, updates, and performance charts available on the TSP website to understand the mechanics, tax rules, and changing legislation.

- For Active Federal Employees: Treat downward market dips as a winning opportunity for your financial success. Continue contributing the maximum amount you can afford during this trend.

- For Retirees: If you are already retired, the best strategy during a sharp market downturn is to do absolutely nothing. Do not panic and sell. Just wait it out.

- Close Your Eyes: Take a deep breath, figuratively close your eyes to the headlines, and let patience carry you through. Focus on your career if you are working, or focus on golf, tennis, and your hobbies if you are retired.

Seeking the Right Advice.

Because the TSP is a self-directed account, the ultimate responsibility falls on you. Today, I see participants seeking financial advice from almost anyone willing to give it. They join Facebook investor forums and ask nonprofessionals how to manage their life savings.

Accepting financial assistance from unqualified strangers poses an immense risk. If you take a bad Netflix or restaurant recommendation from a Facebook acquaintance, your loss is little to none. But if you take their bad financial advice, you may watch your hard-earned money go straight down the drain. Stay away from social media forums.

Again, if you are going to ask someone for advice regarding your retirement, they must meet one of two criteria:

1. They are a fellow federal employee who has actually achieved TSP millionaire status.

2. They are a certified financial professional who possesses specialized knowledge of the TSP and is *not* trying to sell you insurance or annuities.

YouTube is filled with self-proclaimed "experts" who base their entire presentations on basic concepts from *Investing for Dummies* (a book I highly recommend for beginners) but completely fail to understand the intricate rules, forms, and mechanics of the TSP itself.

When I watch a football game, I appreciate hearing a commentator who is a Super Bowl Champion. It gives them instant credibility. You know they played the game, made the sacrifices, and actually achieved their ultimate goal.

After retiring, I launched my own financial coaching business to give federal employees and retirees that exact level of real-world credibility. I help clients navigate their TSP investments, set up outside IRAs, manage brokerage accounts, and achieve their FERS retirement dreams. The greatest compliment I have received lately is when two new clients chose to hire me over a massive firm like Fisher Investments. Why, because while the podcasting financial professionals out there claim to know the federal system, none of them can say they actually rode the rollercoaster, survived their own mistakes, and became a TSP millionaire.

Creating a strong financial profile and reaching the status of a TSP millionaire is a challenging task, but by building a solid foundation, learning the basic mechanics of the plan, and tuning out the amateur noise, the path to the millionaire club becomes as second nature as tying your shoes. Evaluate your entire portfolio, stay optimistic, and just hang on for the ride.

Chapter 5

What should I do with my TSP when I leave federal service?

Whether you are retiring or leaving federal service midcareer for the private sector, you must decide how to handle your TSP. The central question facing many federal employees is whether to maintain their TSP investments with the government or transfer them to an Individual Retirement Account (IRA) brokerage account. Because everyone has a unique lifestyle, risk tolerance, and financial pressure, this choice is rarely easy. Many employees simply want to cut ties with their former employer—a feeling I fully understand. To navigate this difficult situation, we must weigh the positive and negative sides of making this move.

Without question, the TSP is an exceptional 401(k)-style plan. It provides an employer match of up to 5% of employee contributions, a proven 39-year track record of successful growth, and a helpful loan program. It also boasts some of the lowest administrative expenses of any retirement plan. Users can choose between five diverse investment options: the Government Securities Investment (G) Fund, the Fixed Income Index Investment (F) Fund, the Common Stock Index Investment (C) Fund, the Small Capitalization Stock Index Investment (S) Fund, and the International Stock Index Investment (I) Fund.

For distributions, the TSP allows for monthly withdrawals and recently updated its rules to provide greater flexibility. If you do choose to transfer your portfolio outside of the government, you retain the right to move it back into the TSP later. However, you must maintain a minimum balance of $500 to keep this account open; closing your TSP completely in retirement is a final, irrevocable step.

Leaving federal service brings critical logistical challenges. If you exit with pending TSP loans, a crucial policy shift provides a massive relief: you can now continue to repay a TSP loan even after you have terminated federal service, thanks to multiple repayment options. This eliminates the panic many employees feel about paying off a loan prior to termination. However, if you fail to manage these options correctly, or if you are under age 59½ and take an unapproved distribution, you will still face a 10% IRS early-withdrawal penalty.

Furthermore, you must look closely at the realities of the private sector. Throughout my federal career, I occasionally heard presentations from financial companies suggesting that moving funds to an individual IRA provides superior asset control and more investment options. But be careful what you wish for. I once had a client whose 401(k) sat with a reputable private firm; they paid a $1,500 annual administrative fee while receiving zero services, alongside commissions on every mutual fund transaction. Unlike the TSP, which is a self-directed account that never aggressively markets to you, private accounts expose you to the sales pitches of investment advisors. These pitches often push expensive annuities or junk bonds that yield large commissions for the advisor. Worse, you expose your life savings to predatory financial advisors like Bernie Madoff and others who have historically betrayed their clients' trust.

Many employees harbor a deep mistrust of the government, even inventing conspiracy theories that federal agencies will misuse their TSP accounts. Yet, the government has never defaulted on a U.S. Savings Bond or failed to pay a Social Security check. Employees looking for "more control" often pull their money out, only to turn that control over to a private investment manager. While critics at financial seminars argue that TSP investment options are limited, the reality is that you already possess excellent choices and low expenses. To my knowledge, there has never been a single fraud scandal associated with the TSP since its inception.

If you are determined to move your assets to seek alternative withdrawal flexibility or charitable distribution options, remember the age-old wisdom: do not put all your eggs in one basket. Billionaires like Elon Musk, Mark Zuckerberg, and Warren Buffett do not keep their wealth with a single bank or advisor. Personally, my TSP, my IRA, and my wife's IRA are all held with separate custodians (the entities that hold your assets, distinct from your investment managers). Splitting your retirement assets protects you from localized system failures or institutional fraud. Consider that during Fiscal Year 2021, the Securities and Exchange Commission (SEC) received 31,373 investor complaints and questions regarding private financial entities; I do not know of a single SEC complaint ever filed against the TSP.

Before moving a single dollar of your life savings, pause, ask questions, and read the fine print. If you seriously want to transition your TSP to an IRA, select multiple reputable custodians and spread large portions of your portfolio among them. If you are a TSP millionaire, move half to one custodian and half to another. You can execute this step via a TSP direct rollover transfer to an IRA on a partial or full basis without paying any immediate taxes. Meticulously compare their rates of return, custodial fees, and quality of service. Moving cautiously can save you a considerable amount of time, money, and aggravation.

Admittedly, the modern TSP landscape has faced logistical hiccups following a massive website overhaul. The new interface does have some excellent features, including enhanced colors and highly scannable, large fonts that make navigating menus easier. However, the system still lacks the depth of major brokerage houses like Fidelity or Charles Schwab. Shockingly, the platform fails to retain detailed historical transaction data. As a 39-year TSP investor, I should be able to look back four decades at my historical contributions and compound growth, but this data is unavailable. The TSP board spent millions on this contract, yet participants are left with significantly less historical information than the prior legacy website provided.

Even more troubling is how the platform handles complex calculations like Required Minimum Distributions (RMDs). When system errors occur, customer service representatives are frequently unable to explain why forced withdrawal figures do not align with actual account balances. Worse, the TSP has begun taking automated action for individuals who miss their RMD deadlines by printing physical checks and mailing them to the address on file. The checks are mailed due to the TSP investor has not set up a direct deposit regarding their mandatory RMD. In an era of common mail theft, mailing RMD checks worth tens of thousands of dollars to TSP millionaires who may be traveling or staying at their vacation home is an unacceptable risk. The TSP must transition entirely to mandatory direct deposit setups for these withdrawals.

Despite these frustrating platform issues, I strongly caution clients against panic-selling or completely abandoning the TSP due to short-term website friction or market cycles. Having navigated Black Friday in 1987, the DOT-com crash in 2000, the Financial Crisis of 2008, and the COVID pandemic era, I know firsthand that market downturns typically recover within a year or two.

While past performance guarantees nothing, long-term optimism is rewarded.

I have no plans to leave the TSP. While time will tell how many participants ultimately exit out of frustration with the platform's flaws, I remain confident that the platform will eventually be refined to provide the elite level of service and transaction transparency that federal employees desire during their careers and retirement.

Conclusion:

Every federal employee and retiree has the opportunity to become a TSP Millionaire. With nearly 225,000 members among this elite group of investors, you too can join them by taking disciplined, consistent steps throughout your career and retirement.

I remember a folk hero from Massachusetts, named John Chapman who was known as Johnny Appleseed. He traveled the United States and Canada sharing his knowledge of planting apple trees. His legacy was that he was responsible for planting tens of thousands of apple trees and his selfless agricultural education was part of his dream.

My goal is to share my knowledge and experience with TSP investors and wish that they can benefit from them.

I hope this book has been a helpful guide to securing your financial goals.

Good luck!

Appendix A

The Third Million (December 2021):

Appendix B

The Fourth Million (June 2025):

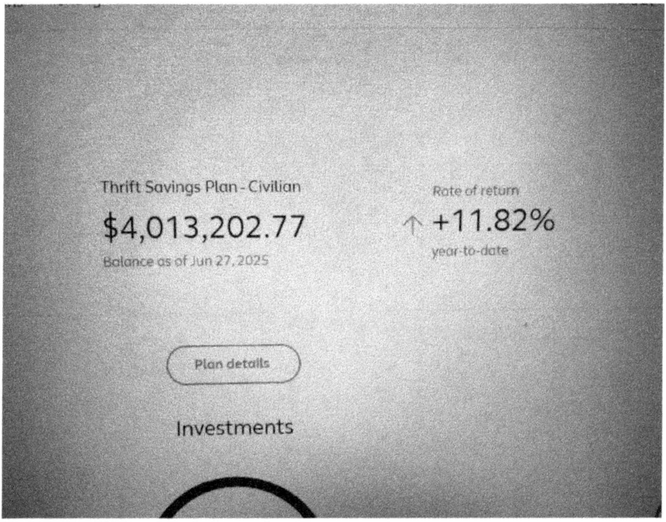

Appendix C

My Fifth Million (June 2026):

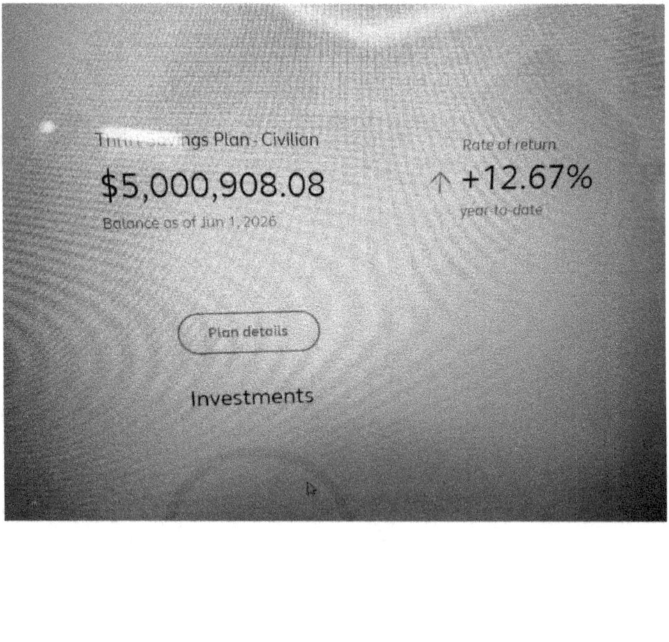